S. Hrg. 113–199

EUROPEAN UNION ECONOMIC RELATIONS: CRISIS AND OPPORTUNITY

HEARING

BEFORE THE

COMMITTEE ON FOREIGN RELATIONS
UNITED STATES SENATE

ONE HUNDRED THIRTEENTH CONGRESS

FIRST SESSION

MAY 23, 2013

Printed for the use of the Committee on Foreign Relations

Available via the World Wide Web: http://www.gpo.gov/fdsys/

U.S. GOVERNMENT PRINTING OFFICE

WASHINGTON : 2014

86–863 PDF

For sale by the Superintendent of Documents, U.S. Government Printing Office
Internet: bookstore.gpo.gov   Phone: toll free (866) 512–1800; DC area (202) 512–1800
Fax: (202) 512–2104   Mail: Stop IDCC, Washington, DC 20402–0001

(II)

CONTENTS

(III)

EUROPEAN UNION ECONOMIC RELATIONS: CRISIS AND OPPORTUNITY

THURSDAY, MAY 23, 2013

U.S. SENATE,
COMMITTEE ON FOREIGN RELATIONS,
Washington, DC.

The committee met, pursuant to notice, at 10:05 a.m., in room SD–419, Dirksen Senate Office Building, Hon. Robert Menendez (chairman of the committee) presiding.

Present: Senators Menendez, Shaheen, Murphy, Corker, and Johnson.

OPENING STATEMENT OF HON. ROBERT MENENDEZ, U.S. SENATOR FROM NEW JERSEY

The CHAIRMAN. Good morning. This hearing of the Senate Foreign Relations will come to order.

This hearing is on the economic relationships between the United States and the European Union. And I want to thank our witnesses who will provide the committee with a deeper understanding of the realities behind the headlines.

Last week, a headline in The Guardian said: "Eurozone Suffers Its Longest Downturn Ever As France Sinks Back Into Recession," the latest reminder that the economies of many European remain quite fragile.

More than 5 years after the start of the worst financial crisis and recession since the great depression, 9 of the 17 Eurozone countries are in recession. The Eurozone as a whole contracted for the sixth straight quarter, the longest in the history of the euro, and the broader 27-member European Union has now also slipped back into recession.

This continuing weakness in Europe clearly has implications here in the United States and not just at a macroeconomic level but for the welfare of banks, businesses, consumers, and workers.

Our cooperation with the EU also has broader national security and foreign policy implications. For decades, our interdependent partnership with EU members has been a key component of efforts to counter global security threats, promote greater democracy, economic openness, human rights, and ensure nations adhere to basic norms and standards. A Europe that is economically compromised and increasingly inward-focused could have grave repercussions for these broader issues.

So I am going to have the rest of my statement entered into the record since we are going to be having votes in a little bit. But I do appreciate two extraordinary individuals to help us with their assessment of the economic turbulence in the Eurozone, the implications for the fragile global recovery, the effectiveness of the EU and multilateral responses, including the critical role the International Monetary Fund has played in supporting fragile European economies.

[The prepared statement of Chairman Menendez follows:]

PREPARED STATEMENT OF CHAIRMAN ROBERT MENENDEZ

Thank you for attending this hearing on the economic relationship between the United States and the European Union and thank you to our witnesses who will provide the committee with a deeper understanding of the realities behind the headlines.

Last week a headline in The Guardian said: "Eurozone Suffers Its Longest Downturn Ever As France Sinks Back Into Recession," the latest reminder that the economies of many European countries remain quite fragile.

More than 5 years after the start of the worst financial crisis and recession since the Great Depression and nine of the 17 Eurozone countries are in recession.

The Eurozone—as a whole—contracted for the sixth straight quarter, the longest in the history of the euro and the broader 27-member European Union, has now also slipped back into recession.

This continuing weakness in Europe clearly has implications here in the U.S., and not just at a macroeconomic level, but for the welfare of banks, businesses, consumers, and workers.

Our cooperation with the EU also has broader national security and foreign policy implications.

For decades, our interdependent partnership with EU members has been a key component of efforts to counter global security threats, promote greater democracy, economic openness, and human rights, and ensure nations adhere to basic norms and standards.

A Europe that is economically compromised and increasingly inward-focused could have grave repercussions for these broader issues.

The United States and Europe have together formed the core of the world economy for at least the last century, and we continue to have the largest trade and investment relationship in the world, with annual flows between the United States and the EU of roughly 1½ trillion dollars of trade in goods, services, and income receipts from investment, responsible for millions of American jobs.

Together we have been the driving force for shaping global standards and regulations, liberalizing world trade, and prioritizing labor, environmental, and intellectual property rights.

And while U.S. foreign policy priorities evolve to account for a changing world, our relationship will keep growing and our futures will be even more intertwined and integrated.

In my view, the EU—and world economies would be in much worse shape were it not for the coordinated regulatory and policy interventions of the G20, IMF, and the Federal Reserve Bank and European Central Bank, and—as I said last week at the Bretton Woods Conference—supporting these efforts was crucial to preserving our own interests.

Faced with enormous challenges in the world we engage, we don't shrink back into our shell, we fix problems, and we find solutions. We realize that we can make a difference on the issues that affect all of us: the interconnectivity of people and nations; the clash between internationalism and isolationism; adapting global economic governance structures to an ever-changing world; and the confluence of economic and national security; and the importance of fostering new democracies.

I think we all would agree that every so often, the United States faces defining moments in foreign policy—when the old order gives way—sometimes painfully, often searchingly—when old rules no longer apply and a new, if unfamiliar, order arises from the chaos.

We and the EU have faced such circumstances in recent years, and we have refused to shrink from our responsibilities.

Today we have four witnesses to help us understand this incredibly complex and vital transatlantic economic relationship.

We have asked them to provide their assessment of the economic turbulence in the Eurozone, the implications for the fragile global recovery, and the effectiveness of the EU and multilateral responses, including the critical role the International Monetary Fund has played in supporting fragile European economies.

We also anticipate hearing from them on opportunities for greater economic and commercial cooperation.

To start the conversation this morning we have: Robert Hormats, Under Secretary of State for Economic Affairs and Lael Brainard, Under Secretary of Treasury for International Affairs.

Both are extraordinarily talented and experienced individuals with distinguished records of public service, and I want to thank both of you for your many years of dedication to advancing the vital national economic interests of the United States. We are thankful to you both for joining us today and look forward to your insights.

Let me remind everyone that after this session we will continue the discussion with two distinguished members from the think tank world, both of whom are experts on the subject of U.S.–EU relations and well-known in their own right—The Honorable Jim Kolbe and Douglas Rediker.

The CHAIRMAN. To start the conversation this morning, we will have Robert Hormats, the Under Secretary of State for Economic Affairs and Lael Brainard, the Under Secretary of the Treasury for International Affairs. Both are extraordinarily talented and experienced individuals with very distinguished records of public service. And I want to thank both of you for your many years of dedication to advancing the vital national economic interests of the United States.

And we will have a second panel as well, which is also very distinguished.

With that, let me turn to Senator Corker for his remarks.

STATEMENT OF HON. BOB CORKER, U.S. SENATOR FROM TENNESSEE

Senator CORKER. Mr. Chairman, thank you and thank you both for being here. I, too, will be brief. I know we want to try to gauge it so we finish this first panel, vote, and come back.

But thank you for being here.

I know that we all understand the financial crisis had a huge impact around the world, not only here but also certainly in Europe. Since that time, they have had economic stagnation. It is my view they really have not addressed the many structural issues that need to be addressed. It has mostly been dealt with through central bankers and other mechanisms. They have really not addressed the things that they need to do. We have some of the same problems here.

But this TTIP is an incredible opportunity for us, and for the transatlantic partnership. I know both of our witnesses on this panel are involved in that. This is an opportunity for all of us. I know my own State and I am sure the States represented here on the dais benefit tremendously from trade between the European Union and the United States. And if we can lower tariff and non-tariff barriers, I know it will be good for both entities and it will create stronger alliances.

We thank you for being here today and look forward to your testimony.

The CHAIRMAN. With that, let me welcome you both. Secretary Brainard, we will start with you.

STATEMENT OF HON. LAEL BRAINARD, UNDER SECRETARY FOR INTERNATIONAL AFFAIRS, U.S. DEPARTMENT OF THE TREASURY, WASHINGTON, DC

Secretary BRAINARD. Chairman Menendez, Ranking Member Corker, and other distinguished members of the committee, thank you very much for the opportunity to be with you today.

The risk of protracted stagnation in Europe is one of the most important challenges currently confronting the global economy. Real domestic demand in the euro area is lower today than at the low point of the global crisis in 2009. Unemployment has reached the highest level in at least two decades, with over half of young people out of work in countries like Spain and Greece.

Euro area leaders deserve credit for the difficult steps they have taken to restore financial stability and address the risk of cascading defaults and exit. Spain and Italy are now able to borrow at rates that are significantly lower than just a year ago.

But one of the lessons of our own crisis is that restoring financial stability, while vital, is just the first step for the economy to heal. Decisive action is needed now to restart demand and avoid the risk of protracted stagnation in Europe.

We welcome discussions at the ECB about additional measures to unclog credit channels for small businesses in places like Spain and Italy. The severe credit crunch in southern Europe is undermining economic activity and weakening the key engine for growth of small businesses.

Second, events in Cyprus only serve to underscore the importance of moving forward now with full banking union to restore confidence and restart credit to starving local economies. An effective, credible banking union should include not only a single supervisory mechanism but also common resolution authority, recapitalization capacity, and credible deposit insurance.

Our experience here in the United States suggests that a strong backstop enhances the credibility of stress tests and permits capital to be built without further damaging deleveraging. Our experience also suggests that orderly wind-down of banks is easier when there is a well-established legal framework for resolution that clearly prioritizes deposits, buttressed by a strong system of deposit insurance and sufficient loss absorption capacity, including long-term bail-in-able debt.

Third, European leaders need to do more to recalibrate the pace of fiscal consolidation to support demand. Our experience suggests that mid-course correction can make a vital difference. Some countries should stretch out the consolidation path, while those with fiscal space should shift to supporting demand. We welcome indications that France, Spain, and the Netherlands will take additional time to meet their targets.

Finally, Europe's surplus countries can and should do more. Increased demand in Europe's strongest economies would provide relief to weaker euro area economies but also help spur the United States and world economy. Where current account surpluses remain above 6 percent of GDP, faster wage growth and greater homeownership can make an important contribution.

The past few years have shown how closely tied are American jobs and growth to financial conditions in Europe and around the world. IMF actions, in particular, have helped shelter the U.S. economy from shocks from abroad, protecting American jobs, exports, and household savings. The IMF has helped our European partners limit contagion and restore financial stability. It has done so primarily through its unmatched technical expertise and credibility. Europe itself is providing the lion's share of the financing.

The IMF is also an important partner in strengthening national security, helping countries from Jordan to Tunisia to Yemen anchor financial stability and undertake reforms.

And finally, when countries join the IMF, they sign up for important obligations to maintain open markets and avoid "beggar thy neighbor" policies. The Fund helps investors better assess risks by setting standards for transparency and data. Countries face censure when they fail to meet those obligations, as is currently the case with Argentina.

As the global economy undergoes a profound reconfiguration, it is more important than ever to renew U.S. leadership of the IMF. That is why we look forward to working with members of this committee and Members of Congress more broadly to expand the core quota resources of the IMF with no net new U.S. financial commitment to the IMF, while preserving the U.S. veto and enhancing its legitimacy. I look forward to working with you on this important agenda.

Thank you.

[The prepared statement of Under Secretary Brainard follows:]

PREPARED STATEMENT OF UNDER SECRETARY LAEL BRAINARD

Chairman Menendez, Ranking Member Corker, distinguished members of the committee, thank you for the opportunity to speak with you today about one of the most important challenges facing the global economy.

The Transatlantic relationship is a critical anchor of America's economic and national security. European allies are essential partners in our strategic engagements around the world, from the historic changes underway in the Middle East and North Africa to addressing Iran and North Korea. U.S. financial and trade linkages with Europe are strong, and we hope to make them stronger still by moving forward with an ambitious Transatlantic Trade and Investment Partnership agreement.

But even as our own economy continues to heal, U.S. companies are adversely affected by weak business and consumer demand across Europe. Three years into the euro area crisis, the risk of protracted stagnation represents one of the most important challenges to the global economic outlook.

Since the beginning of the crisis, President Obama has actively engaged with European leaders, urging action to restore financial stability and support growth. Secretary Geithner and Secretary Lew have shared experiences from our own crisis response and recovery plan, emphasizing the importance of addressing market challenges decisively and retaining flexibility to calibrate monetary and fiscal policy to the pace of recovery.

Euro area leaders deserve credit for the difficult steps they have taken to restore financial stability and address the risk of cascading defaults and exit. Spain and Italy are now able to borrow at rates that are significantly lower than they were a year ago.

Now the focus must shift from stabilization efforts to supporting demand growth in order to avoid protracted stagnation and address record levels of unemployment, especially among Europe's young people.

Since the end of World War II, European leaders have been engaged in a historic project to build a closer union. At the birth of the euro over a decade ago, political leaders understood they were making a choice with historic consequences when they permanently ceded control over monetary policy and exchange rates. Europe's crisis has confirmed that monetary union without the requisite fiscal and financial integration leaves the euro area vulnerable.

Looking back at the creation of the euro, it is clear that some risks were anticipated, while others were not. Fiscal risks were broadly anticipated, but no mechanism for fiscal risk-sharing was created to address unexpected shocks. Financial integration was identified as a goal, rather than flagged as a potential risk, allowing the growth of large-scale banks with extensive cross-border linkages without commensurate centralization of supervision and resolution authority.

And the extensive debate that took place on the creation of the euro largely ignored the risk of external imbalances within the euro area. Even today, while large external deficits are flagged as risks, there is little discussion of how addressing surpluses in countries that export substantially more than they import might help ease the sharp compression of demand now underway in deficit countries.

It was very significant when we saw the European Central Bank (ECB) and European leaders join together in support of a strategy anchored by critical financial commitments to ensure that countries undertaking reforms retain access to market financing and to assure banks have access to liquidity and hold credible capital. These commitments decisively boosted confidence and restored stability to financial markets.

One of the lessons of our own crisis is that restoring financial stability, while critical, is just the first step for the economy to heal. The focus of the policy debate in Europe must now shift from restoring financial stability to developing a plan to boost demand and employment.

Domestic demand in the euro area is now lower than at the low point of the global crisis in 2009 in real terms. All of the recovery in European output since that time has come from net exports. That is not sustainable for a region that accounts for almost 20 percent of the world economy.

In 2012, demand contracted by over 2 percent across the euro area. Unemployment has reached the highest level in at least 20 years with over half of young people out of work in countries such as Spain and Greece. This poses political risks no less than economic risks.

Decisive action is needed now to restart demand and avoid the risk of protracted stagnation.

First, we welcome discussions on strengthening credit access for small and medium-sized enterprises in southern Europe. The severe credit crunch in southern European countries is undermining economic activity and weakening the small business sector, traditionally a major engine of job creation. In the face of weakening growth and continuing disinflation, we welcome the ongoing discussion at the ECB about additional measures to improve the transmission mechanism and address elevated borrowing costs and unclog credit channels for small businesses in southern Europe.

Second, events in Cyprus only serve to underscore the importance of moving forward with full banking union. Europe is making progress on the single supervisory mechanism, but it cannot stop there. An effective, credible banking union should include not only a single supervisory mechanism but also a common resolution authority, recapitalization capacity, and credible deposit insurance. Banking union requires some degree of risk-sharing between members.

The upcoming bank stress tests and asset quality reviews are a critical opportunity to restore confidence in bank balance sheets and restart credit to starving local economies. Our experience suggests that the credibility of stress tests is enhanced when there is a strong backstop in place, permitting capital to be built without a further downward spiral of deleveraging.

We also have learned from our own experience that it is much easier to wind down banks in an orderly manner when there is a well-established legal framework for resolution that clearly prioritizes deposits, buttressed by a strong system of deposit insurance. There must be sufficient loss absorbing capital as well as long-term debt that can be bailed in.

In addition, European leaders should do more to recalibrate the pace of fiscal consolidation. As we know from our experience, course correction can make an important difference. Recent evidence has shown that continued sharp fiscal consolidation risks further undermining demand, especially when the scope for conventional monetary easing is limited. The consolidation path should be stretched out in some countries, and those with fiscal space should shift to supporting demand. We welcome indications that France, Spain, and the Netherlands will be given additional time to meet their budget targets, but there is room to do more in the near term.

Finally, surplus countries should contribute more to demand. Rebalancing is hard to sustain when it rests wholly on the compression of demand in deficit countries. Increased demand in Europe's strongest economies would not only provide relief to weaker euro area economies, but would also help spur the world economy. In countries where current account surpluses remain above 6.0 percent of GDP, spurring private demand in areas such as faster wage growth and greater homeownership can make an important contribution.

For our part, the U.S. recovery is gathering strength by the day. But over the past few years we have seen how closely tied American jobs and growth are to financial conditions in Europe and around the world.

During these years, we have seen in concrete terms the value of the International Monetary Fund (IMF) in protecting America's economic and national security.

When financial conflagrations have broken out among our trading partners, the IMF has acted as the first responder; it has built firebreaks to limit contagion even as it has helped our trading partners stabilize and heal their economies. The IMF's actions have helped shelter the U.S. economy from headwinds abroad and protect U.S. jobs, exports, and the savings of American households.

The IMF has helped our European partners stabilize and strengthen the foundations of their monetary union over the past 3 years. We have been closely engaged through the IMF and directly in encouraging European leaders and the ECB to put in place a joint strategy buttressed by a strong firewall to enable countries to undertake necessary reforms, while cleaning up bank balance sheets and ensuring ample liquidity. The primary value of the IMF's close engagement has been through technical expertise and credibility; Europe itself is providing the lion's share of the financing. The IMF is now calling for Europe to implement a strategy to boost demand and combat unemployment, which is important not only for Europe but also for recovery in the United States and the world.

The IMF is an important partner in strengthening our national security. The IMF is now helping to address longstanding impediments to sustainable and inclusive growth that are essential in securing democratic transitions in Arab Spring countries such as Tunisia and Yemen and to anchor economic stability in countries such as Jordan and Morocco.

The IMF helps to enforce transparency and strengthen market discipline. It plays a central role in setting norms and standards for the smooth functioning of the market-based system of international trade and finance that is at the core of U.S. prosperity and stability. This creates new opportunities for U.S. businesses as they expand and sell products to new markets overseas, which supports additional jobs here at home.

As the global economy undergoes a profound reconfiguration, with new economic powers increasingly exercising their influence, it is more important than ever for us to renew our leadership of the international financial system. That is why we have asked Congress, in the President's budget, to safeguard U.S. leadership in the IMF by approving the 2010 quota and governance reforms. The budget proposal will expand the core quota resources of the IMF—with no net new U.S. financial commitment to the IMF—while preserving the U.S. veto and enhancing the legitimacy of the institution. Today, U.S. approval is the only remaining step needed for these important reforms to go into effect.

At its founding, the United States had more influence on the IMF's design and operations than any other country. Today, it is vital we safeguard our influence in the face of rapid shifts in the global economy, working together to strengthen demand and growth in Europe and here at home.

The CHAIRMAN. Thank you, Madam Secretary.
Secretary Hormats.

STATEMENT OF HON. ROBERT D. HORMATS, UNDER SECRETARY FOR ECONOMIC GROWTH, ENERGY AND THE ENVIRONMENT, U.S. DEPARTMENT OF STATE, WASHINGTON, DC

Secretary HORMATS. Well, thank you very much, Mr. Chairman and Ranking Member Corker. I want to also express my thanks to other members of the committee who are very actively involved in our United States-European relations for their attendance as well.

I want to thank you, Chairman Menendez, for calling this important hearing at a very important time.

My testimony—the written testimony—offers a fuller discussion of some of the economic details of our relationship, and Under Secretary Brainard has emphasized a number of very key points about Europe's current economic circumstances.

I would like to just utilize a brief oral testimony to make a few basic points, one of which is that we have seen our relations with Europe and the trade and the economic area, really since the end of World War II, be very closely intertwined with our strong and highly important strategic and political relationship. The two reinforce one another. And this has really been true since the Marshall Plan, since the creation of the OECD and even the Kennedy Round, all of which were meant as economic measures that would enhance our economic ties with Europe, but they also underpinned a broader political and security relationship. And I think we have the opportunity to do the same thing now. While economics is the critical important element of our relationship with Europe with respect to, say, TTIP, it also can strengthen ties between our two countries in a variety of other areas.

And the key point is we need Europe in many, many ways. From the point of view of addressing international threats, there are a host of challenges where the United States and Europe have worked together in the past and need to continue to work together, and closer economic cooperation can underpin that relationship. And a prosperous Europe that is able to utilize its resources both to address domestic problems and also to work with us to address global security issues and global economic issues is a very important part of our foreign policy and our national security policy as well.

What we are trying to do in TTIP, in particular, is to build a 21st century transatlantic relationship that meets the needs of Americans and Europeans together and address a wide range of new issues, many of which have not been dealt with or have not been dealt with in a complete or satisfactory way in other negotiations. So this is really the most ambitious negotiation we have ever had, and I would say if you add TTIP plus the TPP—the Trans-Pacific Partnership—negotiations, this is probably the most and I would say certainly the most historic opportunity for improving the global trading system since the Kennedy Round. We have an opportunity not only to expand trade opportunities but to improve the rules on which international trade is based for our own countries and also if we do this in the correct way, we can encourage the buy-in of third countries to the kinds of rules that we work out with the Europeans or we work out, in the case of TPP, with the Asians.

So the stakes here are enormously high, and they are enormously important in part because if the United States and Europe can identify good rules and good standards and utilize them amongst our own economies, we will be able to have a greater degree of job creation within our economies. But we will also speak with a much stronger voice when we negotiate with many of the emerging economies of the world—many of whom do not see the world trading system or the rules of the trading system in the same way, divided or much weaker—in convincing these countries to make the kind of changes that we want in order to create a level playing field in a united sense. If we can pull together, we are in a much stronger position to do that. And because these countries are the largest and fastest growing markets in the world today, when you add them all up, helping our own economic opportunities or enhancing our own economic opportunities will enable us to strengthen our prospects for getting a level playing field amongst these other countries as well. So that is a critically important area.

As you know, we have a number of areas, over 20 different areas, that we have identified and were sent up in a letter to the Congress by Ambassador Marantis, areas where we have particular objectives. The Europeans have their objectives as well. And our hope is that we will be able—even though we recognize these are tough issues and many of them have been tough for quite some time, we are quite aware of how difficult this negotiation is, but we are also aware that the stakes are very high. The stakes are high, in terms of strengthening our economic relations, using our stronger economic relations to strengthen our political and security relations, and also using this as an opportunity to enable us, the United States and Europe, to be in a stronger position to convince other nations to engage in rules and standards and procedures which will level the playing field for our companies and have a more effective global trading system.

[The prepared statement of Under Secretary Hormats follows:]

PREPARED STATEMENT OF UNDER SECRETARY ROBERT D. HORMATS

Thank you, Chairman Menendez, Ranking Member Corker, and other distinguished members of the committee for inviting me to testify today on the U.S.–EU economic relationship.

The strategic alignment between the United States and Europe, rooted in shared history and values, has never been closer in addressing both international threats and opportunities—and a host of internal challenges.

U.S. ties with Europe evolved significantly during the 20th century. After the Second World War, America's leaders recognized that our common future—not just Europe's future—depended on Europe's economic recovery from the war, and of course that of Japan. That the Marshall Plan combined security with a strong economic dimension is why it got such strong support in the United States.

During the cold war, shortly after the advent of the European Economic Community, we together initiated the Kennedy Round of trade negotiations in 1964. The Kennedy Round had aims that included increased United States-European trade. More broadly it sought to sharply reduce global tariffs, break down farm trade restrictions, and strip away some nontariff regulations. It also sought to boost trade with developing nations.

At the time we also saw the Kennedy Round as part of the broader goal of strengthening the transatlantic partnership—one that might ultimately lead to a transatlantic economic community. And in that respect, the Transatlantic Trade and Investment Partnership—if it achieves its ambitious goals—might be seen as the culmination of the spirit that animated the Kennedy Round.

Although cold war thankfully is over, our work in strengthening United States-European relations is not. There is no other region with which the United States shares more broadly the same values, and no other region with whom partnership, alliance, and shared goals is achieved so readily. Among our central goals for this relationship continues to be to further enhance our mutual prosperity. Today, we draw on the same common values and same shared interests build a 21st century transatlantic economic partnership that meets the needs of Europeans and Americans in this new century and serves as a beacon for the rest of the globe

We are building on what those before us began. For us and for coming generations of Americans and Europeans, the compelling argument for strong transatlantic ties cannot be rooted in past disputes, but must be future-oriented, based on jobs and economic growth, and on shared values of democracy, respect for diversity, freedom of speech and religion and expression, and on shared opportunity.

TRANSATLANTIC TRADE AND INVESTMENT PARTNERSHIP, (TTIP)

One of the most exciting portions of President Obama's State of the Union Address was the announcement of our intention to negotiate a Transatlantic Trade and Investment Partnership, or TTIP. This heralds a new era in the transatlantic relationship. The TTIP will be a challenge, but one worth undertaking. Already excitement is building on both sides of the Atlantic about the potential for this potentially wide-ranging agreement.

The economic relationship between the United States and Europe is already strong and integrated. The United States and the European Union together have 812 million consumers. And the United States exported $458 billion in goods and private services in 2012 to the EU, our largest export market.

Companies in the United States and the European Union have invested a total of over $3.6 trillion in each others' markets and approximately 50 percent of total U.S.–EU trade is intracompany. U.S.–EU trade and investment already supports an estimated 13 million jobs on both sides of the Atlantic.

A successful Transatlantic Trade and Investment Partnership could further strengthen and deepen U.S.–EU trade and investment ties. A comprehensive agreement between the United States and the European Union also would have positive effects throughout the global economy. Strengthened economic ties between the United States and the European Union, and the benefits they produce for both of our economies, will enhance our ability to build stronger relationships with emerging economies in Asia and elsewhere around the world—relationships that support high quality norms and rules in the global economic system.

With tariffs between the United States and the European Union already low, our trade negotiators will aim to address "behind-the-border" barriers to U.S.–EU trade, including unnecessary regulatory and standards differences that create burdens for our exporters, while maintaining appropriate health, safety, and environmental protections. If we and the EU are successful in addressing these "behind-the-border" issues, we can expect to see the benefits of this cooperation spread to other markets.

Let me dwell for a moment on the reasons for this. Companies that sell in the transatlantic market want to maximize production efficiency by minimizing the number of different requirements to which they must conform. U.S.–EU regulatory cooperation will thus improve our own production efficiency—but it can also improve product quality and safety in many markets and thus in the goods we import. And it can promote a more level playing field for American companies in third markets.

U.S.–EU regulatory cooperation—and the adoption of such cooperative outcomes by other countries—can also help integrate the United States, Europe and other established economic powers with a new group of rapidly emerging economic actors—such as China India, Brazil, Russia, and others—based on procedures and high standard rules for successful market—oriented commerce.

ENERGY

I'd also like to take a moment to discuss energy. The United States and the EU also have an enormous interest in each other's energy security and promoting cooperation and research on emerging energy technologies and policies, related to such things as smart grids, critical materials, and e-mobility. They have a robust energy dialogue under the U.S.–EU Energy Council headed by the Secretaries of State and Energy. Many EU Member States have heightened their focus on renewable energy technologies. And the EU as a whole has established ambitious energy efficiency targets.

At the same time, we've seen many American companies invest heavily in Europe, not just in the traditional hydrocarbon industry, but also in unconventional gas, renewable, and alternative energy opportunities.

U.S. and EU researchers also are collaborating on many leading-edge technologies, such as those that will enable electric vehicles to connect to the grid on both sides of the Atlantic. We are also working together to increase our knowledge of the critical materials required for certain renewable energy technologies, and identifying ways to make us less reliant upon imports of these materials and to use them more effectively.

Before concluding, I would like to make a final point. The rebalancing of U.S. foreign and economic policy to Asia has received much attention of late. But, as Vice President Biden remarked in Munich in February, our engagement with Asia is in Europe's interest and does not come at Europe's expense. Europe remains, as the Vice President noted, America's indispensable partner of first resort. Indeed it is profoundly in Europe's interest for the United States to engage more broadly with Asia. It is also worth mentioning that Europe has engaged in a broad range of new trade and investment activities in Asia as well.

There is no denying the economic importance of Asia. It is an enormous economic priority for the United States—as it is for Europe. Indeed, I believe that both Europe and the United States will be in a stronger position to meet the competitive challenges of Asia if we have stronger economic ties with one another and if we agree on high common standards.

This larger and more systematic approach that we are undertaking now can make a big difference. Let me emphasize here that, as with past trade negotiations, the success of TTIP will depend on sustained and enthusiastic leadership from the President and his counterparts in Europe. And I believe we have and will continue to have both. It will also depend on very close cooperation with the Congress and constituencies throughout the United States. The same types of coordination must take place within Europe utilizing Europe's own institutional structures. I believe these are also well in train.

None of this will be easy. But while the challenges are great, the opportunities are even greater. This is, in many respects, a once-in-a-generation opportunity to reshape our relationship with the European Union. I believe that an agreement is achievable and that it can strengthen the relationship between the European Union and the United States—both economically and politically—for many years to come.

I thank the committee for this opportunity to draw attention to the important issue of U.S.–EU economic relations and I look forward to answering your questions.

The CHAIRMAN. Great. Well, thank you both. For the record, your full statements will be included in the record without objection.

So let us explore some of the items you have raised. Let me start with you, Secretary Brainard. Last week, I spoke at the annual meeting of the Bretton Woods Committee. You know, one of the things I believe is that the United States worked to create the IMF to help create stability in global financial markets, and for roughly six decades, the IMF has played a critical role and continues to do so in responding to economic and financial crises. And I think through its actions and through our leadership, it has preserved American jobs, helped prevent economic crises from creating political instability and escalating to armed conflict and therefore threatening our national security.

So I heard you make some references to the IMF. I am interested in your thoughts as it relates to what role—has it played a stabilizing role in responding to the Eurozone crisis. Its involvement has not been without controversy, obviously. What is the administration's assessment of the IMF's role in the Eurozone crisis to date, and how important has its participation been in supporting mostly EU-led stabilization efforts?

Secretary BRAINARD. Well, thank you, Mr. Chairman.

I think the IMF's role within the euro area, as they have navigated this crisis, has been nothing short of critical for protecting the world economy, limiting contagion, helping restore stability, and helping avoid much more fundamental instability that could otherwise have occurred. And by doing so, the IMF, working together with euro area leaders, has helped protect U.S. household savings, jobs, exports here.

They have done that primarily through the technical expertise that they bring to the table, as well as the credibility—the credibility among market participants, as well as among the authorities—and they have helped the Europeans craft programs that strike a better balance in terms of supporting the recovery, have helped Europeans take very decisive actions on their banking system, similar to the ones that we took here. And they have done it by providing a minor share of financing. So if you look at the financial packages that have been necessitated, in some cases the IMF's contribution has been $1 for every $5 that has been provided by the euro area.

Our role in the IMF, as you have pointed out, our leadership role, has allowed us to also participate in those conversations through the IMF, and our influence in the IMF I think is at no time more important to safeguard given the broader shifts in the global economy.

The CHAIRMAN. And in that context, let me just follow on your last comment there. Is our leadership at the IMF at risk, given that we are the only major IMF member that has not approved the 2010 governance and quota reforms?

Secretary BRAINARD. Well, I think the fact that we are the only thing standing in the way of the IMF completing the quota and governance reforms is something that over time could erode our standing.

The other thing that I think is very important is if we do not go forward and reinforce the core quota resources of the Fund, which are really at the center of the Fund's activities, the IMF will increasingly rely on ad hoc bilateral loan arrangements that other countries are happy to provide because they view these as simply an alternative place to hold their reserves. And so I think our influence could be severely eroded over time if we allow those ad hoc arrangements to become the primary way the IMF funds itself.

The CHAIRMAN. Secretary Hormats, a final question for you. Some say the Eurozone crisis could turn EU governments to focus inward, limiting the extent to which we can partner with the EU in a variety of foreign policy issues. When we look at noneconomic issues—obviously, the economic issues are pretty compelling, but on the noneconomic issues, is there a risk here of that becoming a reality?

Secretary HORMATS. Yes, there is a risk, and I think it is a risk that we need to be aware of. You have phrased it, I think, quite accurately that countries that face economic difficulties at home or resource constraints at home find it more difficult to get political support or to obtain the resources that they need for international activities.

We have been working very closely with members of NATO, in particular, when it comes to the security side to avoid that turn of events, and also we are working with them to try to rationalize the way NATO forces are structured and NATO arms are procured so that they get more efficiency per unit of money expended for their resources. But we are very cognizant of this, and we have had an ongoing dialogue with members of NATO to try to minimize the degree to which essential support for NATO efforts and for financial support for NATO are continued even during this crisis because the world—even though countries go through crises and difficulties, threats do continue, and therefore, we and other NATO countries need to be prepared for this. And we are working very closely to minimize the cuts and also to rationalize the use of resources so that we get more bang for our buck, so to speak, within the NATO context.

With respect to foreign assistance, much the same thing. There are cuts but the cuts so far—because there is a lot of political support in many of these countries for foreign assistance, we have not seen large cuts, but nonetheless, there is a pull-back in some countries, very substantial pressure for more pull-backs.

The CHAIRMAN. Thank you.

Senator Corker.

Senator CORKER. Thank you, Mr. Chairman.

And thank you both for your testimony. I did not realize we were going to have a commercial today for the IMF, but I know that every time I see Lael that is going to happen.

Christine LaGarde was up the other day meeting with several of us. And I will say that the quota resources issue is going to come to a head soon. I do hope that you will socialize that issue with many Members. I think this is an issue on which there is not a lot of understanding. I do think it is going to take some effort. It is not just going to come up for a vote and be passed. But anyway, thank you very much for being here.

Mr. Hormats, with TTIP, I assume that we begin the process with everything being on the table. Right? We are discussing every single issue.

Secretary HORMATS. Yes.

Senator CORKER. We are not excluding on the front end any issues?

Secretary HORMATS. That is correct. Our goal is to have as broad a mandate as we can on our side, and we also are encouraging the Europeans to do the same, that is to say, we do not want them to take things off the table in advance of the negotiations. If we did that, then there would be a lot of constraints on the ability to get the kind of ambitious outcome that we would like to get.

Senator CORKER. So, Secretary Brainard, my understanding is that there maybe a push by Treasury to take some of the financial regulation issues off of the table. I know you talked about some of those. But my sense is that issues relative to derivatives, issues relative to some of the Volcker Rule issues may be taken off the table and that the administration will try to negotiate outside of the agreement we are talking about. I just wondered if you would weigh in on that.

Secretary BRAINARD. Senator Corker, the issue of financial services in the TTIP—obviously, recognizing that we are still in stakeholder consultation process, so we are still hearing from stakeholders. But, of course, financial services, while you would expect would be in, we think that there are important market access gains that we would push for, and, of course, we want to nail down some market access that we have gotten but have not gotten committed.

With regard to regulatory convergence, as you know better than anybody, Senator, we have obtained commitments not just from Europe but from all G20 members, from all Financial Stability Board members, to bring their standards to the levels that our regulators are now implementing. And we have obtained commitments to do that in very tight timelines. Most of those are intended and committed to be done this year. We think it is extraordinarily important, as our regulators move forward to implement the very important financial reforms that responded to the ravages of the crisis, that we not disadvantage our companies by moving forward in a way that leads to an unlevel playing field.

So I would say that our most important focus has to be getting the whole set of countries in the G20, not just the Europeans but very important Asian markets, to implement on time, and that will be mostly in the next few months.

Senator CORKER. But are you taking those issues outside of TTIP is the question because I understand there is a very big push-back by the European countries regarding those two issues I just brought up. And my question is, Are you going to try to take those off of the table, which could lead to Europe taking agriculture off the table and possibly other kinds of sensitive issues.

Secretary BRAINARD. I think our focus, quite the reverse, is to not give our European counterparts any excuse to slow down the implementation that they have already committed to in areas like bank capital, on resolution, on cross-border derivatives, on clearing, on the full set of commitments they have made. We want to make sure that we see implementation on timeframes that will put our players, our market participants, on a level playing field. And those timeframes are very immediate. So we are going to continue to put a focus on getting that implementation.

Senator CORKER. Do you think they will be done in advance of reaching an agreement on TTIP?

Secretary BRAINARD. They have committed to have them done on a timeline that is more ambitious. And we are going to continue to push for those timelines because they were important concessions that we want to see implemented.

Senator CORKER. Thank you.

Mr. Hormats, I know this administration has a lot at stake in the auto industry. There was a recent study that indicated if you could do away with the nontariff barriers to the auto trade, under this agreement, it would be the same as taking a 27-percent ad valorem tax off of the industry. And I am hoping that the administration is committed to knocking those barriers down to zero so that we can make sure we do not have duplicate regulation taking place. I would love to hear your comments in that regard.

Secretary HORMATS. Well, we have actually paid a great deal of attention to the auto industry as we have begun to develop our own positions on this. In fact, we have had this very useful comment period over the last several months where we have gotten a lot of comments from the auto industry, and many of them have been directed at just the points you have raised with respect to tariffs, but particularly the nontariff barriers which are a major issue. You are quite correct. If we can reduce these what we call ''behind the border'' measures, which tend to be regulatory issues, standard setting issues, and develop a level of consensus which ends up in much lower barriers to transatlantic trade in this sector, it could be of enormous benefit.

We have actually worked in another group, the Transatlantic Economic Cooperation group, or TEC, to help the auto industry work together, in effect, on electronic cars and reduce differences in standards and regulations quite considerably so that the opportunity for greater transatlantic trade in automobiles, in hybrid cars or electronic cars, is now considerably greater than it was, but our aim is to do similar things here. We think there is great opportunity for reducing regulatory barriers to trade in many things, and the auto sector would certainly be a very strong candidate for that.

Senator CORKER. Thank you both for your service. I appreciate it.

The CHAIRMAN. Senator Murphy.

Senator MURPHY. Thank you, Mr. Chairman. Thank you for this hearing.

I appreciate both of our witnesses' focus on TTIP. As the chairman of the Subcommittee on European Affairs, we hope, through the committee, to be able to be on the leading edge of explaining the benefits of this agreement, one that will be very complicated to Members of the Senate.

Mr. Hormats, I want to ask you to focus on a portion of your testimony that you did not necessarily spend time on in your verbal remarks with respect to energy.

Secretary HORMATS. Yes.

Senator MURPHY. When the Turkish delegation was here about a week ago, they spent a good deal of time—at least a portion of their members did—trying to convince us of the importance of LNG exports to that region. Anytime you talk to the Poles—who have some degree of consternation over the last several years of missile defense announcements—they understand that perhaps the most important thing we can do for them is to help them, diversify their energy supply as well.

I want you to talk for a second about what we can do not only to try to diversify the energy sources in Turkey, but also in Eastern Europe so that there is less reliance on places like Russia and Iran, and particularly with respect to LNG exports. This is something that all of Europe, not just that region, are certainly looking forward to. If you can talk a little bit about the future of U.S. energy policy specifically with respect to those regions?

Secretary HORMATS. Yes. Thank you very much for asking it.

This is a vitally important part of our overall relationship with Europe today, in large part because of the reasons that you have just mentioned. And that is, we want to help the Europeans to diversify their sources of energy, the kinds of energy they utilize, and the way in which it is delivered in order to give them a greater degree of variability in the way they decide on when and how to procure energy. That is to say, we do not want them to be in a position where they get the largest portion of their energy from one source because that source may or may not be reliable all the time and may ask for pricing provisions, which are much greater than might be available through other methods.

So what are we doing? We are trying to develop, among other things, alternative pipeline routes to Europe for both oil and gas, the southern routes in particular. We are encouraging the Europeans, now that we are importing less natural gas from Qatar because we have our own gas boon—more of that is going to Europe. We are working with Europe on a number of areas of shale gas or alternative gas development. We have a number of projects in alternative energies, wind and solar in particular. So we have a very strong ongoing effort with the Europeans to help them diversify energy sources.

And what we have seen already is actually quite impressive. I mean, even though they have not really moved directly into shale because it takes time to develop the technology, we have seen as a result of their ability to access alternative sources of energy a far stronger European position in negotiating natural gas contracts with Russia. Russia used to have an arrangement whereby the natural gas price was linked to the oil price. Now, in the past, they really had no choice but to go along with that. Now they do because while the price of oil is quite high, there are many new sources of natural gas available.

With respect to American natural gas, we have a process of approval of project by project, but in some of those projects, there will be opportunities, I believe, for Europeans to access American natural gas, but it will depend on the Department of Energy's individual decisions with respect to specific projects.

Senator MURPHY. I want to ask one question with respect to TTIP, and that is this: There are essentially two negotiations that are going to be taking place; one between the EU and the United States and one within the EU. And one of the things that we overlook is that there is going to have to be a significant degree of harmony amongst those nations in order to negotiate what is likely the biggest trade agreement that they have ever tried to undertake as a unit.

So I pose the question to both of you very quickly: Are we underestimating or overestimating the degree to which one of the most problematic aspects of this agreement will be the ability of the EU nations to get on the same page, especially with respect to these nontariff barriers?

Secretary HORMATS. Well, you are quite right. There are those two negotiations.

The Europeans now are in the process of developing their mandate and the mandate effectively is a negotiation which is led by the European Commission but involves 27 member governments, and they are now trying to work this out themselves and try to get a consensus, or as close to a consensus as they possibly can, among those governments for the open mandate that we are asking for and that the Commission wants. They do not want a lot of constraints on their ability to negotiate. So they are working that through, and by the middle part of June, this is supposed to be resolved and worked out. And so far there is reason to believe that while there are pressures by certain governments to get certain things off the table, so far the Commission, I think, has done quite a good job. And I think the governments realize that a negotiation with the United States, if they take too much off the table on their side, their ability to get the kind of things they want in the negotiations is also constrained by that approach. So, so far I think things have worked well, but we will not know candidly until we get their mandate, which will be in 2½ weeks.

The CHAIRMAN. Senator Johnson.

Senator JOHNSON. Thank you, Mr. Chairman. I would like to thank the witnesses for being here.

Under Secretary Hormats, let us go back to TTIP. In your testimony, you show that currently our exports to Europe is $458 billion and that they are the largest export market. Are we their largest importer or have we been surpassed?

Secretary HORMATS. Collectively—well, China—yes, we are. We and Europe have the biggest bilateral trade both ways of any two areas.

Senator JOHNSON. Good. So we have not been eclipsed.

In terms of the issues, I would like to do it from the United States side and then from the European perspective. What are the top three trade barriers that we are experiencing that we are going to be negotiating over? In what product areas or what issues?

Secretary HORMATS. We are trying at this point not to get too specific about what our individual negotiating objectives are, but let me give you a general idea of what the concerns are and where we will be focusing. And I think if you have a chance to take another look at the letter Ambassador Marantis just sent up, you will get a sense of that.

But basically the key areas are the ones that have been mentioned earlier. Many of them are nontariff barriers which have to do with regulations. The regulations in many cases relate to agriculture, and coming from Wisconsin, your farmers are familiar with a lot of these agriculture-related issues. So overall, nontariff barriers are probably the most important element of this.

Senator JOHNSON. That is from the U.S. perspective.

Secretary HORMATS. From the American perspective. That is right.

Senator JOHNSON. So that is our primary complaint. What is their primary complaint against us?

Secretary HORMATS. Well, they would like to see a number of things. I mean, we have things like the Jones Act. We have a number of things where they would like to see some of our laws and regulations modified so some of their companies could play a greater role in the United States, things of that nature. So there are a wide range of specific issues. The tariffs on light trucks as a result of a historical set of events are quite high; 25 percent. Some of their light truck companies would like to get that.

But they are mostly in the areas of standard setting. They would like to see our standard setting and their standard setting converge. And I think if you were to identify the central point of a discussion between our two countries, it is to try to find a way of ensuring that American regulatory standards and the procedures by which those standards are set are more transparent. And each side has the opportunity to play a greater role in trying to develop a convergence.

This is not to say that we want to lower the barriers of the quality of the regulations. We want to make sure that the regulations meet the safety needs of the American people, and the Europeans want to do the same. The question is whether we can find ways of doing it in a way which is mutually consistent and does not deter trade or interfere with trade. That is really the center point of it. And we can go through case and verse.

At the end of the 90-day period, we will have a clearer idea of where we are going to come out and where they are going to come out on the specifics. At this point, it is a bit harder to get into the specifics. But those are at least some of the very important areas.

Senator JOHNSON. So it really sounds like both sides have the exact same complaint against the other. It really does break down in which product area.

Secretary HORMATS. It largely is the same set of concerns, that if you can have common standards and common regulations and common procedures for developing those standards and regulations, then there is an opportunity for a more seamless set of trade relations between our two countries.

But the other element that can be as important in the long run is if we can agree on common high standards that meet the needs of our people, then there is an inducement for other countries to adopt those standards. A, we are in a stronger position to push them than we would be if we are divided. But, B, if you are a producer in, say, India, you are going to say to your government, we do not want to have to comply with Indian standards and then the Euro-American standards. So there will be pressure in those countries to adopt these increasingly global standards, and in turn, if they do that, then American companies that are trying to sell in these countries will encounter fewer barriers as well because there will be a greater possibility of internationalized standards as opposed to balkanized ones.

Senator JOHNSON. Just one real quick question. Has the administration put a number or a goal, and if we succeed in coming to an agreement, what that would mean in terms of additional exports?

Secretary HORMATS. We have not done that exactly, but we have been utilizing a lot of data that we have received from various economic think tanks and other groups that have made very clear calculations on the amount of trade that can be produced, the benefits for GDP growth on both sides, and the benefits for job creation. I will be very happy to send you some of their data, which is quite good. I mean, they are not all the same, but they all point to a much more positive direction for——

Senator JOHNSON. Do you want to quick throw out one of those numbers just to whet our appetite?

Secretary HORMATS. I have got them. Let me go through and I will come up with them in a second.

Senator JOHNSON. That is fine.

Thank you, Mr. Chairman.

Secretary HORMATS. But I will make sure you get them.

The CHAIRMAN. Thank you very much.

Let me just follow up very quickly. We have a vote going on. I know Senator Corker has a final comment for this panel.

In response to your questions of Senator Johnson about what is the core of the essence of the negotiation, I just want to—because I know some of the sentiments of some of the members here, as well as some of the sentiments of some of the Members in the Senate, and that is that harmonization does not mean necessarily subversion of sovereignty. Right? Secretary Hormats?

Secretary HORMATS. Pardon me?

The CHAIRMAN. You were looking for the figures. You can get it to Senator Johnson and you can provide it for the record.

I just want to make sure because I know sometimes our colleagues have concerns here. So your response to Senator Johnson's question about what is the essence of the TTIP negotiation—and so I just want to make sure so that we have a fully included record that harmonization does not necessarily mean subversion—it does not mean subversion.

[EDITOR'S NOTE.—The information requested for the record had not been provided at the time this hearing went to press.]

Mr. HORMATS. It does not. On the contrary, it means we want to make sure that the standards—our goal in setting the standards and regulations is essentially to make sure that we protect the safety of the American people when, for instance, we are talking about safety regulations.

The CHAIRMAN. As well as our economic interests.

Mr. HORMATS. And certainly as well as our economic interests.

The CHAIRMAN. So it does not necessarily entangle us. It enhances our abilities.

Mr. HORMATS. Absolutely. The goal is to do two things: one, to protect our interests but also to enhance prospects for greater export opportunity to these countries. And that is our goal.

One of the concerns—and let me elaborate because I think you made a very important point. One of the things we are very focused on is that when regulations are established in particular areas, they be based on scientific evidence as opposed to being done for political purposes. So we want to make sure that science-based evidence is available when decisions are made, for instance, on various types of agriculture regulations, which is very important for a number of products that the United States sells. And the same thing with cars. It is not just putting where the light ought to be. It is having a real reason, when you make that regulation, for doing it. So we want evidence-based decisions when it comes to regulations.

The CHAIRMAN. I appreciate that response.

Senator Corker.

Senator CORKER. Again, thank you.

And I just want to make one brief comment too. I really appreciated Senator Murphy's comments about the energy piece. And, Secretary Hormats, I was recently in Munich meeting with a number of business leaders there. The energy policies that Germany in particular, but many European countries, have generally put in place have also created a tremendous opportunity for foreign direct investment here in the United States to produce products that are going to be shipped back to Europe because of the tremendously competitive energy prices we have.

I know that he is still looking for that number. I hope he is listening to the comment.

Secretary HORMATS. I am for sure.

Senator CORKER. Senator Johnson has gotten you all fouled up here, I know. But would you comment on that? Is that not a tremendous opportunity for this country if we can get this agreement done? We have an opportunity for those manufactured products to be built here and shipped back to Europe because of the tremendous natural gas prices that we have here.

Secretary HORMATS. Absolutely. One of the dramatic revolutions that we have had in this country is in the area of natural gas and also tight oil, which is in North Dakota and Montana. But the natural gas revolution, the fracking revolution some would call it, is very important because it does two things. One, it has dramatically lowered the price. Second, it has made us much less reliant on imports because I mentioned earlier we used to import Qatari gas. Now we do not need to do this. And it is a highly valuable asset from our point of view.

What is also interesting, Senator Corker, is that if you look at a lot of American companies today, the notion of outsourcing used to be very attractive. Now, when you add two things together—one is the availability of natural gas on a very steady basis in different parts of the country, and two, a lot of countries are concerned about the length of their supply chain. As chairman of GE Immelt put it, he likes to have, now, more visibility over his supply chain. So we are beginning to get circumstances in which people are coming into the United States or reconsidering the export of manufactured goods to other parts of the world. So this is a very important benefit.

There is the huge price differential. If you take the price of natural gas delivered to Asia, LNG, it is probably three times higher than the price of LNG gas at Henry Hub, which is the place where the market effect is created here. It costs a little bit more to move it around from there, but basically we have a big differential. And it is a very good thing for throughput for plastics companies, for instance, but also for people who utilize that gas for power. And gradually our hope is that this will back out other sources of energy and enable us to utilize the gas to a much greater degree.

And we also are much more efficient than we were years ago in the utilization of both gas and oil.

Senator CORKER. Thank you both.

The CHAIRMAN. Well, thank you both for your testimony. We look forward to continuing to be engaged with you on these issues.

The committee will stand in recess so that we can vote. The chair's intention is to vote, immediately come back, and call up our second panel.

[Recess.]

The CHAIRMAN. The committee will come back to order.

I want to thank our panelists for their forbearance as we had votes. And I know that both of you understand that, especially Congressman Kolbe.

I am pleased to begin our second panel related to our topic of the United States and the European Union economic relations. We have two distinguished members from the think tank world today who will give us further insight into the economic challenges and opportunities facing Europe and the United States.

The Honorable Jim Kolbe currently serves as the senior transatlantic fellow for the German Marshall Fund of the United States. We know him well here in Congress because he served with great distinction for over 20 years in the House of Representatives representing the State of Arizona.

The Honorable Douglas Rediker is a visiting fellow at the Peterson Institute for International Economics. He previously represented the United States on the Executive Board of the International Monetary Fund.

And both of these gentlemen have extensive experience working on issues related to the European Union and are experts on the subject of United States-European Union economic relations.

So let me thank you both for being here today, and with that, I will recognize Congressman Kolbe.

STATEMENT OF HON. JIM KOLBE, SENIOR TRANSATLANTIC FELLOW, THE GERMAN MARSHALL FUND OF THE UNITED STATES, WASHINGTON, DC

Mr. KOLBE. Thank you, Mr. Chairman, Senator Corker. It is a pleasure to be with you and the members of the committee here today.

I will submit my entire testimony for the record and I will summarize it here very briefly.

The CHAIRMAN. Without objection, both of your statements will be fully included in the record.

Mr. KOLBE. Thank you, Mr. Chairman.

It is a great opportunity to appear before the committee today, and I think it is appropriate that the committee is holding this hearing on the current economic situation in Europe and the potential opportunities that the United States and the European Union might share that could generate economic growth.

I think we all know that Europe is coping with the most difficult crisis it has faced since the Second World War. It is struggling with the financial crisis that began, to some extent here, in 2008 and has now turned into a severe economic and employment crisis.

A prolonged recession could be corrosive to the foundations of the European Union. For the past 5 years, we have witnessed the effects of a persistent and deep recession in Europe. Tensions can quickly turn into anger and resentments toward the EU as populations in the southern countries express resentment toward a range of policies which they believe are placing asymmetrical economic pressures upon them. If these perceptions are not reversed, the economic recession in Europe could very well undermine the legitimacy of more than half a century of EU political and economic integration.

The United States has played an important role in Europe affairs serving as the offshore balancer since the early 20th century, but for the last decade, we have adopted more of a role as an observer rather than a full participant. We viewed economic events in Europe through a prism of how economic problems in Europe might affect our own economy. We have adopted an attitude that this is a problem to be solved by Europe and Europeans. Undoubtedly, it is certainly true that the United States cannot impose a solution on Europe but, nonetheless, we have an important stake in helping resolve the economic and financial crisis in Europe.

The EU is our largest and most important trading partner. I know you have heard this already this morning. Combined, we account for nearly half of the world's GDP. The United States and the European Union account for nearly a third of global exports and imports. And foreign directed investment is an important component of job creation and represents a long-term commitment on the part of the investor to the receiving country. Over $100 billion in foreign direct investment came from the European Union to the United States in the year 2011 alone. In fact, nearly half of all the current FDI to be found in this country originates in the EU.

However, our relationship goes far beyond strong economic ties. We share a deep and abiding commitment to Western values of openness, rule of law, free markets, and democracy. We share deep security ties through NATO. Simply put, we are heavily invested in each other's success.

The economic malaise in Europe has a direct impact on these strategic links that tie the United States and Europe together.

A persistent economic recession in Europe, if not reversed, threatens to undermine the very foundations of the EU and the process of EU integration with far-reaching results. If Europe is unable to reinvigorate growth and opportunity in the southern tier, it risks fracturing this consensus surrounding the benefits of European integration. Southern Europe is likely to see only the suffering and hardships of austerity and little of the benefits that might flow from continued EU membership.

For the United States, this prospect of a fraying political and economic consensus in Europe poses a difficult dilemma. The United States has derived important national security benefits from a prosperous and unified Europe.

Assume for a moment that Europe is consumed by a vicious cycle, struggling with increasingly severe economic problems and a fraying political consensus. Strategic challenges may develop on the international scene and the United States and European Union could find themselves unable to mount a unified response.

What, as a policy matter, can the United States do to take the sting out of the economic crisis in Europe? I think that the United States and the EU can work together to take steps that assist Europe in weathering its current crisis while laying the foundation for the long-term growth.

Of course, I am talking about TTIP, the Transatlantic Trade and Investment Partnership. It has the potential for being a vitally important trade and investment agreement which can benefit both economies, but it should also be viewed as being in our strategic interests.

TTIP will directly benefit the United States in several ways.

First, it can renew and rebuild the historic United States-European Union relationship.

Second, TTIP will demonstrate to southern EU member states and to the United Kingdom new benefits to EU membership.

Third, United States and European Union cooperation on TTIP will deliver benefits on the economic global stage. Because of its sheer scope and its size, TTIP can help overcome trade fatigue and spur efforts to remove trade barriers around the globe. It can provide a strong incentive for advancing rules-based trade liberalization. If fashioned properly, it can provide an open door through which other countries can walk and join in an ever-widening circle of countries committed to trade liberalization.

Let me suggest just very briefly, because I realize my time is up, just two ground rules that I think TTIP must meet if its high expectations are to be set for it.

First, it must be ambitious. The negotiation should begin by being as comprehensive as possible. There should not be any attempt to leave off one thing after the other. They should take the position that everything is on the table for discussion. Do not take sensitive sectors out of the negotiations before we even begin.

And second, it should have a strong focus on regulatory convergence and equivalence. The real gains from the agreement will come not from eliminating tariffs, but from eliminating nontariff barriers. To use the example of automobiles, the same car produced in the United States and Europe is subjected to different safety and environmental testing, even though the regulatory outcome is virtually identical. These different testing rules, which lead to the same safety and environmental outcomes, add significantly to the costs of the overall product and limit our competitiveness. Achieving a workable process for our industries to develop mutual recognition on regulatory development should be a top priority in any negotiation.

Mr. Chairman, members of the committee, this is the moment for the United States and Europe to negotiate the boldest, broadest trade and investment agreement we have ever contemplated since World War II. The time is ripe. The will is there. The benefits for all are obvious.

Thank you, Mr. Chairman.

[The prepared statement of Mr. Kolbe follows:]

PREPARED STATEMENT OF JIM KOLBE

Mr. Chairman, members of the committee, thank you for the opportunity to appear before the committee today. Europe is our most important ally and certainly our largest trading partner, so it is appropriate that the committee is holding this hearing on the current economic situation in Europe and potential opportunities the United States and the EU might share that could generate economic growth.

In 2011 and 2012, I cochaired the Transatlantic Task Force on Trade and Investment, a joint project by the Swedish Trade Ministry, the European Centre for International Political Economy (ECIPE) and the German Marshall Fund of the United States (GMF.) In our report, issued in February 2012—in the middle of a growing Euro-crisis in Europe and a deep economic recession here at home—we concluded that the time was ripe to move forward with a new transatlantic trade and investment agenda to promote economic growth, jobs, innovation, welfare, and economic development. I am pleased—as are all the other members of our task force that the Obama administration and the European Commission will soon commence formal negotiations for a free trade agreement along the lines we advocated.

Europe is coping with the most difficult crisis it has faced since Second World War. But it is a crisis not brought on by the machinery of war, but by the inadequacy of its economic and financial machinery. The EU is struggling with a financial crisis that began in 2008 and has now turned into a severe economic and employment crisis. Europe's attempts to cope with its sovereign debt and ensure bank solvency to stabilize the financial system have shown some success, but high unemployment and social instability remain with signs of worsening ahead.

A prolonged recession could be corrosive to the foundations of the EU. For the past 5 years, we have witnessed the effects of a persistent and deep recession in Europe. Tensions have risen between the relatively prosperous northern countries in Europe and those struggling in the south as leaders at both ends pull different levers in an effort to bring stability to the economic system and restore growth. As we have seen in recent elections and in street demonstrations—in Italy, Spain, Greece—tensions can quickly turn into anger and resentment toward the EU as populations in the southern countries express resentment toward a range of policies which they believe are placing asymmetrical economic pressures upon them. Over the long haul, if these perceptions cannot be reversed, the economic recession in Europe could very well undermine the legitimacy of more than half a century of EU political and economic integration.

The United States has played an important role in Europe affairs, serving as the "offshore balancer" since the early 20th century. For much of the 20th century, the United States considered its strategic relationship with Europe to be the most important in the world. Bretton Woods, the Marshall Plan, NATO, the IMF and the World Bank all stand as monuments to that deep relationship. But for the last decade and particularly as the European economic crisis deepened, the United States has adopted more the role of an observer, rather than a full participant.

To the extent that the United States viewed economic events in Europe as a matter of serious concern, it has done so primarily through a prism of how economic problems in Europe might affect our own economy. Largely because of our own fiscal and financial difficulties, we have adopted an attitude that this is a problem to be solved by Europe and Europeans. While it is certainly true that the United States cannot impose a solution on Europe and a lasting solution must have its origins with Europeans, the United States nevertheless has an important stake in helping resolve the economic and financial crisis in Europe.

Europe's economic troubles affect us directly and deeply. The fact is, using any of several different measures, the United States and Europe constitute the most important economic relationship to be found in the world today.

The EU is our largest and most important trading partner. Combined, we account for nearly half of the world's GDP. The U.S. and E.U. account for nearly a third of global exports and imports.[1] In fact, Europe purchased 3 times as much of our exports as did China and 15 times more than India. Looked at from the European side of the window, the United States purchased twice the amount of European goods as they sold to China and nearly seven times the quantity sold to India.[2]

An equally important measure of the relationship is to be found in foreign direct investment. FDI is an important component of job creation and represents a long-term commitment on the part of the investor to the receiving country. By this measurement, it is clear that Europe and the United States look favorably upon each other as an opportunity for investment. Over $100 billion in Foreign Direct Investment came from the European Union to the United States in 2011 alone. In fact, nearly half of all the current FDI to be found in this country originates in the EU. Likewise, the United States invested an estimated $150 billion in the EU in 2012. Because the United States and the EU are advanced economies, much of this investment supports intrafirm trade—international flows of goods between parent companies and their subsidiaries or affiliates in another country. And it is here that the greatest opportunity lies for increasing our already substantial trade.

However, our relationship goes far beyond strong economic ties. We must not underestimate the importance of the strategic, political, and cultural relationships that bind us together. We share a deep and abiding commitment to Western values of openness, rule of law, free markets, and democracy. We share deep security ties through NATO, arguably the most successful alliance in history. Simply put, we are heavily invested in each other's success.

The economic malaise in Europe has a direct impact on these strategic links that tie the United States and Europe together.

A persistent economic recession in Europe, if not reversed, threatens to undermine the very foundations of the EU and the process of EU integration with far-reaching results. For example, the countries of southern Europe are young democracies, many born as recently as the 1970s. The peoples of these nations rejected an authoritarian past as they looked northward for inspiration to a unified Europe that was democratic, strong, and prosperous. Even today, EU membership is a strong attraction to many former Soviet bloc nations in eastern and Central Europe, and others on the periphery, like Turkey, as these countries either reorient their economies away from a Soviet-managed economic system or to manage conflicting national identity issues. The EU provided a means of transcending these conflicts, many of them centuries old, as EU membership give their citizens a sense of belonging to a unified Europe. They also view membership in the EU as a source of economic opportunity as they join a continent-wide, internal market, free of tariff and other barriers that continue to stunt intracontinental trade in such regions as East and West Africa or Southeast Asia. If Europe is unable to reinvigorate growth and opportunity in its southern tier, it risks fracturing this consensus surrounding the benefits of European integration. Southern Europe, struggling with high unemployment and economic uncertainty, is likely to see only the suffering and hardships of austerity and little of the benefits that might flow from continued EU membership.

For the United States, this prospect of a fraying political and economic consensus in Europe poses a difficult dilemma. The United States has derived important national security benefits from a prosperous and unified Europe. Europe has been an important ally of the United States economically, politically, and militarily. The United States, working in concert with a strong Europe, has had the ability to leverage and project our influence and our shared Western values. With increasing integration of the EU, Europe will continue to develop and strengthen its own institutions of parliamentary and federal democracy. This contributes to a virtuous cycle whereby Europe builds and strengthens internally. A Europe which can better organize its internal affairs will be better able to act in concert with the United States in external affairs.

But assume for a moment that Europe is instead consumed by a vicious cycle, struggling with increasingly severe economic problems and a fraying political consensus. In such an environment, strategic challenges may develop on the international scene, and the United States and EU could find themselves unable to mount a unified response. For example, the United States has real interest in Europe's ability to address security problems emanating from North Africa. But if the Mediterranean tier of European Union countries turns its back on economic and political integration, meeting such challenges would be difficult at best. Similarly, Russia could take advantage of EU weakness and take a more assertive role in Eastern Europe. Or on the economic front, the United States and Europe might find itself unable to mount an effective response to growing Chinese assertiveness in Africa and Latin America.

What, as a policy matter, can the United States do to take the sting out of the economic crisis in Europe? I believe the United States can have a positive role in working with the EU as it moves toward growth and prosperity. The United States and EU can together take steps that both assist Europe in weathering its current crisis, while laying the foundation for long-term growth.

As you know, in February, the United States and EU announced their intentions to begin negotiations on a comprehensive, high-standard free trade agreement—the Transatlantic Trade and Investment Partnership, or TTIP for short. I believe TTIP has the potential for being a vitally important trade and investment agreement which can benefit both economies. But we should also view it as being in our strategic national interests.

Trade liberalization is at the heart of the EU project. In 1951, the Treaty of Paris, signed by France, Germany, Italy, and the Benelux states (Belgium, the Netherlands, and Luxembourg) created a common market for coal and steel. This alliance—the stepchild of the visionary Frenchman, Jean Monnet—developed into the European Economic Community and, later became the European Union. Since its creation, the EU has undergone several more iterations of integration—notably the Masstricht Treaty creating the euro currency and the Lisbon Treaty refining and expanding the EU political institutions. What began as a way of drawing the continent of Europe together in peaceful trade and economic development after the horrors of the wars of the early 20th century has become a pathway to deep political integration.

The Transatlantic Trade and Investment Partnership—TTIP—will directly benefit the United States in several ways. First, it can renew and rebuild the historic U.S.–EU relationship and draw the United States and EU even closer together. For four decades of cold war and two-plus decades that have followed, the United States has benefited from a unified and prosperous Europe. A stable and peaceful Europe, a deeply integrated economy, and a shared commitment to democracy provides the United States with a strong and focused partner that helps to promote a common approach to political and military challenges as they arise in other parts of the world.

Second, TTIP will demonstrate to southern EU member states and to the United Kingdom new benefits to EU membership. The U.K. is engaged in a robust debate over its future in Europe with Prime Minister Cameron calling for a referendum on the future of the U.K.'s participation in EU integration. TTIP will provide a powerful incentive for the U.K. to consider favorably its position in the EU since they would draw on the benefits of trade liberalization flowing from TTIP.

Third, U.S.–EU cooperation on TTIP will deliver benefits on the economic global stage. As we noted in our report on Transatlantic Trade Leadership, U.S. and E.U. still lead the world when it comes to global economic policymaking. This position is likely to remain for many years to come. Historically, the United States, European Union, and Japan led multilateral trade talks. While other countries such as China, India, and Brazil are catching up in terms of their economic influence, the U.S.–EU partnership is indispensable to provide global leadership on trade liberalization. Because of its sheer scope and size, TTIP can help overcome "trade fatigue" and spur efforts to remove trade barriers around the globe. This is particularly important in the wake of the stalled Doha round of WTO negotiations. TTIP can provide a strong incentive for advancing rules-based trade liberalization. If fashioned properly, it can provide an open door through which other countries can walk and join in an ever-widening circle of countries committed to trade liberalization.

The TTIP trade agreement is unlike any other we have ever tried. It is unprecedented in its scope. It will be the largest FTA ever attempted and it will be an eye-to-eye negotiation among equals. It will require the significant attention, time, and resources of the entire U.S. Government. We are not just negotiating solely with EU Commission; in effect, we are negotiating with 27 EU countries, each of whom will present unique challenges.

Let me suggest a couple of ground rules for TTIP if it is to meet the high expectations that are being set for it.

It should be ambitious

The negotiation should begin with an eye to being as comprehensive as possible. There are certainly sensitive sectors on both sides of the negotiating table. The United States has longstanding demands with respect to agriculture, such as how to handle the issue of genetically modified organisms (GMOs). The French have already indicated a demand for a "cultural exception" which would preserve restrictions on U.S. imports of movies and television. Europe as a whole wants to pry open the vast market of 50 states' government procurement codes. Both sides should take the position that everything is on the table for discussion; don't take sensitive sectors out of the negotiations before we even begin or we will end up with an agreement that disappoints us all.

It should have a strong focus on regulatory convergence and equivalence

While tariff barriers in both the United States and Europe are low (averaging in the 3–5 percent range with some notable tariff peaks), complete elimination of tariff barriers will provide significant economic gains given the sheer size of our trading relationship. But the real gains from the agreement will come from eliminating nontariff barriers (NTBs). To use an example in automobiles, the same car being produced in the United States and Europe is subjected to different safety and environment testing, even though the regulatory outcome is nearly identical. These different testing rules which lead to the same safety and environmental outcomes add significant costs to the overall product and, ultimately, to the consumer, placing our industries at a competitive disadvantage. One study commissioned by the European Commission indicated that these NTBs are equivalent to an ad valorem tariff of approximately 26 percent.[3] It is the American consumer who pays that tax. Achieving a workable process for our industries to develop mutual recognition on regulatory development should be a top priority for both sides in any negotiation.

Mr. Chairman, members of the committee, this is the moment for the United States and Europe to negotiate the broadest, boldest, trade and investment agreement that has ever been contemplated since World War II. The time is ripe. The will is there. The benefits for all are obvious.

I commend you for holding this hearing. I urge you to keep the pressure on the administration, our negotiators, and all the special interest groups for the next several months to be certain we do not falter and that the outcome is no less tomorrow than what we contemplate today.

End Notes

[1] Source: Hamilton, D. and Quinlan, J. (2011) The Transatlantic Economy 2011, Center for Transatlantic Relations.

[2] Source: "A New Era for Transatlantic Trade Leadership, a Report From the Transatlantic Task Force on Trade and Investment," February 2012, European Centre for International Political Economy and the German Marshall Fund of the United States, page 16.

[3] ECORYs Nederland BV, "Non-Tariff Measures in EU–US Trade and Investment: An Economic Analysis", p. 48, 12/11/2009, cited by the Auto Alliance, May 10, 2013, comments submitted to the U.S. Trade Representative.

The CHAIRMAN. Thank you.
Mr. Rediker.

STATEMENT OF HON. DOUGLAS REDIKER, VISITING FELLOW, PETERSON INSTITUTE FOR INTERNATIONAL ECONOMICS, WASHINGTON, DC

Mr. REDIKER. Thank you, Mr. Chairman and Ranking Member. It is an honor to once again appear before you this morning.

I would like to start my testimony with two reminders.

First, the EU is qualitatively and quantitatively our strongest global ally. It is based on, as we just heard, a set of shared values, including rule of law, openness, property rights, democracy, and for the most part, market economics. The transatlantic economy generates $5.3 trillion in commercial sales each year and employs up to 15 million workers on both sides of the Atlantic. European-controlled companies in the United States employed roughly 3.5 million Americans in 2011. An economically strong Europe is in our national interest.

My second reminder is that the European Union is fundamentally a political project. Although the euro is obviously an economic instrument, its introduction remains principally an outgrowth of political motivations. Perhaps paradoxically to understand European economic issues, one needs to always remember to look primarily through a political prism.

European leaders often note that their progress should be viewed as one would a marathon and not a sprint. By that standard, it is early in the race and there are significant hurdles still ahead.

Europe currently suffers from a broken monetary transmission mechanism, a dearth of available credit, lingering concerns about potential exits from the euro, fragmentation across the European Union, and a negative feedback loop between banks and sovereigns.

While borrowing costs have stabilized in large part due to aggressive action by the ECB, the short-term economic outlook for Europe remains dim, with an expected 0.1-percent decline in GDP across the EU predicted for this year.

So while the worst economic outcomes have been averted, Europe today suffers from stagnation, high unemployment, and a banking system in serious need of shoring up.

Now, in spite of this assessment, the European response over the past 3 years has actually been far more aggressive, effective, and positive than is generally acknowledged. Europe today is significantly more stable and prepared for future events than virtually anyone could have predicted 3 years ago.

Over that relatively brief time span, Europe has created a permanent rescue fund, with up to 500 billion euros available for program countries; created a temporary rescue fund, with an additional 200 billion euros available and already utilized in programs for several countries; seen the ECB expand its limited mandate to heighten focus on the stability of the financial system; undertaken significant fiscal, structural, and financial sector reforms in multiple countries; and reached an agreement on the creation of a single banking supervisory mechanism. This progress has been painful and remains insufficient. But 3 years ago, each of these steps would have been seen as politically, legally, or economically impossible.

Now, with respect to the IMF, its involvement in the euro crisis was initially resisted by many leaders in European countries in part because it was seen as too technocratic and not politically malleable enough to play a constructive role. It could not be counted on to succumb to political pressures to avoid politically unpalatable outcomes. And yet, the IMF's unparalleled expertise led to its inclusion in the troika, along with the European Commission and the ECB, which together have led the crisis response.

Perhaps the most important contribution made by the IMF was as the principal driver of program design, surveillance, and review. And when the IMF did provide financial support, it did so with strict conditionality and with strong support from its executive board.

This is not to say the IMF performed flawlessly. At times, the Fund sent confusing messages on the great economic debate of our time, colloquially known as "austerity versus spending." And the IMF accepted assumptions in the initial Greek program that were proven woefully incorrect. But even then, the IMF played a crucial and positive role. When a country's economic survival is in question, even the IMF needs to balance its role as honest truth teller with the risk of triggering the very consequences that everyone seeks to avoid.

Now, for Europe, as with any marathon, the race does not get easier as it progresses. It gets harder. The issues looming ahead are daunting. They involve the potential for stronger countries to find themselves taking on the risks of weaker ones with the potential quid pro quo of asking those seeking support to agree to rule changes that could include the loss of some element of national sovereignty. This presents a delicate and potentially destabilizing dynamic, putting Germany and France, the two most important founding members of what is today the EU, on a path toward increasingly uncomfortable conflict.

Now, to conclude, while frustrating, inefficient, complicated, and often painful to watch, the evolution of the European Union is something that we as Americans should continue to encourage. While I do not wish to belabor the marathon analogy, those who complete the race often cite the encouragement they receive from those cheering them on along the way. It is in our national interest to remain invested and engaged in Europe's success.

Thank you.

[The prepared statement of Mr. Rediker follows:]

Prepared Statement of Douglas Rediker

Thank you, Mr. Chairman, Ranking Member, and members of this committee. It is an honor to once again appear before you this morning on the subject of United States-European economic relations.

The European Union is a Marathon Political Project

While the purpose of today's hearing is not to rehash what led to the economic challenges currently facing the European Union, I would like to start my testimony with a reminder that the European Union is fundamentally a political project. Although the euro, as a common currency, is obviously an economic instrument, its introduction within the European Union remains principally an outgrowth of political motivations. Somewhat paradoxically, to understand European economic issues, one needs to always look primarily through a political prism.

The introduction of the euro was one step in an ongoing political project intended to ultimately lead to deeper and wider integrated Europe, largely based on a set of basic values consistent with our own. While frustrating, inefficient, complicated, and often painful to watch, the evolution of the European Union is something we, as Americans, should encourage. Its future success serves our direct economic, financial, and strategic interests.

European leaders often note that their progress should be judged as one would in viewing a marathon and not a sprint. By that standard, it is still early in the race, and there are significant hurdles still ahead.

Current Economic Challenges Facing the EU

More than a decade after monetary union, Europe currently suffers from:
- A broken monetary transmission mechanism, in which the traditional tools of monetary policy fail to reach the real economy;
- A dearth of available credit, which hinders real economic activity;
- Lingering concerns about potential exits from the euro, thereby increasing sovereign borrowing costs and increasing overall investment risks;
- Fragmentation, not only within the European Union, but within the euro area itself, with borrowing costs, political tensions, unemployment and growth prospects increasingly diverging into distinct camps—the very opposite of what monetary union was intended to accomplish; and

- A negative feedback loop between banks and sovereigns, in which countries rely too heavily on banks to help finance their sovereign debt, risking a deterioration in the banks' own balance sheets if the quality of that debt is called into question, potentially leading to the need for the already weak and overly indebted sovereigns themselves to step in and provide capital to keep the banking system afloat.

While sovereign and bank borrowing costs have stabilized, in large part due to aggressive action by the European Central Bank, the short-term economic outlook for Europe appears dim, with the IMF predicting an economic decline of 0.3 percent for the euro area this year [1] and the European Commission itself predicting 0.4 percent decline in the euro area and 0.1 percent decline across the EU.[2]

In short, while the worst economic outcomes have so far been averted, Europe today suffers from economic stagnation, unreasonably high unemployment and a banking system that is in need of serious shoring up.

EUROPEAN POLICY RESPONSES SO FAR

In spite of this sober assessment, the European response over the past 3 years has actually been far more aggressive, effective, and positive than has generally acknowledged. That does not mean that there are no further risks. But Europe midway through 2013 is significantly more stable and prepared for future events than virtually anyone could have predicted 3 years ago.

Over that relatively brief time span, Europe has:

- Created a permanent rescue fund, the European Stability Mechanism (''ESM'') with 500 billion euros potentially available for program country bailouts;
- Created a ''temporary'' rescue fund, the European Financial Stability Facility (''EFSF''), with an additional 200 billion euros still available, having already been utilized in programs for three countries within the Euro area;
- Seen the European Central Bank expand its mandate to include, de facto, the preservation of the stability of the financial system, through various standard and nonstandard measures, including the expansion of its balance sheet to over 2.5 trillion euros;
- Undertaken significant fiscal, structural, and financial sector reforms in Greece, Ireland, Portugal, Spain, Italy, Cyprus, and beyond; and
- Reached agreement on the creation of a single banking supervisory mechanism under the auspices of the ECB.

This progress has been painful, has come at enormous political, economic, and social cost, and is far from sufficient. But we would be remiss in not recognizing that 3 years ago, each of these steps would have been seen as politically, legally, or economically unlikely or impossible.

THE ROLE OF THE IMF

The involvement of the IMF in the euro-crisis was initially resisted by many leaders in European countries. In part this was because the IMF was seen as too technocratic and not politically malleable enough to play a constructive role. Perceived as an unyielding technocratic economic institution, the IMF could not be counted on to succumb to political pressures and avoid politically unpalatable outcomes. And yet, the IMF's unparalleled expertise in program design, surveillance, monitoring, and implementation led to its inclusion in the ''troika'' along with the European Commission and the ECB, which together have led the crisis response.

While the IMF provided financial support for several European countries that accepted international programs, the main value added by the IMF in the euro-crisis was as the principal driver of program design, monitoring, surveillance, and review. It was this unparalleled expertise, more than specific financial commitments, that has provided the IMF with disproportionately large influence relative to its financial outlays over the outcomes in Europe thus far. Nevertheless, it is worth noting that in those instances when the IMF did agree to provide financial support, it did so with strict conditionality and with virtually unanimous support from its executive board.

Beyond specific country programs, the IMF has played an influential role on specific and broad policy matters, including research and recommendations on issues relating to banking and financial sector reforms, tax policies, and a wide array of other macroeconomic and structural areas. In short, throughout the euro-crisis, the IMF has served admirably as an independent economic policy advisor.

This is not to say that the IMF performed flawlessly. It did not. The IMF undoubtedly could have done things better. At times, the Fund sent confusing or conflicting messages on the great economic debate of our time—colloquially known as "austerity versus spending." The IMF accepted questionable assumptions in the initial Greek program—assumptions that were proven woefully incorrect. But even in these instances, I believe that the IMF played a crucial and positive role. With a country's economic survival in question, even an international financial institution needs to balance its role as "honest truth teller" with the risk of triggering the very consequences everyone seeks to avoid.

FUTURE PATH FOR THE EUROPEAN UNION

Today's Europe is both fragile and in the process of reinvention. Whether by design or crisis, today's Europe is already greatly evolved from only a few years ago, with even more significant steps toward deeper integration still ahead. Next month, European leaders are expected to formally agree to the creation of a single banking supervisory mechanism under the auspices of the European Central Bank, slated to become operational next year. This is the first step toward full banking union across the euro area. Next steps along this path include Europewide bank asset quality reviews, bank stress tests, the creation of a single bank resolution mechanism and potentially a single resolution fund and a cross-border bank deposit guarantee scheme.

But, as with a marathon, the race does not get easier as it progresses, it gets harder. These looming issues involve both the potential for countries with strong balance sheets to find themselves taking on the risks of those with weaker ones and the potential quid pro quo of asking those seeking outside support to agree to rules and potentially treaty changes that could alter the shape of what it means to be a member of the EU. The potential for a loss of some element of sovereignty in return for financial support remains a delicate and potentially destabilizing dynamic. It puts Germany and France, the two most important founding members of what is today the EU, on the path toward increasingly uncomfortable conflict.

WHY DOES EUROPE MATTER TO THE UNITED STATES?

Quite simply, the European Union represents the most important strategic, financial and economic partner this country has. While there may be times when we grow impatient watching Europe's marathon, we need to recognize how deeply intertwined and invested we each are in each other's success. The emergence of fast growing markets in Asia, Latin America, and Africa are of enormous strategic and economic interest to the United States. Yet, the ties between Europe and the United States remain quantitatively and qualitatively in a league of their own.

Europe remains our strongest global ally. The EU is based on concepts of: rule of law, openness, respect for property rights, democracy and, for the most part, market economics. We clearly have our differences. But, make no mistake. An economically strong Europe is in our national interest.

The transatlantic economy generates $5.3 trillion in total commercial sales each year, employs up to 15 million workers on both sides of the Atlantic.[3] The United States and Europe are each other's primary source and destination for foreign direct investment, with Europe representing 56 percent of total U.S. global FDI since In 2012 alone, U.S. FDI in Europe exceeded $206 billion.[5] Americans invested more in Germany alone than in all of Central America . . . including Mexico.[6] European investment in the United States amounted to $1.8 trillion in 2011, more than 70 percent of total FDI in the United States. In 2011, Europe's investment flows to the United States were seven times larger than to China.[7] The transatlantic relationship also supports American workers, with European-controlled companies in the United States employing roughly 3.5 million Americans in 2011.[8] The EU represents 22 percent of the world's GDP and over 25 percent of global consumption.[9]

CONCLUSION

The euro-crisis represents an opportunity to reform and restructure the EU. While I don't wish to belabor the marathon analogy, those who complete the race often cite the encouragement they receive from those cheering them on along the way. It is in our national interest to remain invested and engaged in their success to ensure that Europe emerges stronger from this crisis.

End Notes

[1] http://www.imf.org/external/pubs/ft/weo/2013/01/.

[2] http://ec.europa.eu/economylfinance/eu/forecasts/2013lspringlforecastlen.htm.

[3] "The Transatlantic Economy 2013," Daniel S. Hamilton and Joseph P. Quinlan, Center for Transatlantic Relations, page 1.

[4] Ibid. page 2.

[5] Ibid. page 2.
[6] Ibid. page 4.
[7] Ibid. page 7.
[8] "The Transatlantic Economy 2013," Daniel S. Hamilton and Joseph P. Quinlan, Center for Transatlantic Relations, page 12.
[10] "The Transatlantic Economy 2013 Volume 1/2013." Daniel S. Hamilton and Joseph P. Quinlan, Center for Transatlantic Relations, page v.

The CHAIRMAN. Thank you both for those insights.

Let me start off where you both ended, Mr. Rediker, in your statement about looking at the EU through a political prism. So what is the focus? From their perspective, what is the focus of that political prism from your view?

Mr. REDIKER. I think whether it is the euro as a currency, which is the most recent manifestation, or the broad expansion and deepening of the European Union, while it has obviously economic consequences, the main motivation was—I mean, go back to the post-World War II era—to create a Europe where armed conflict was never going to be a relevant consideration. And if that is the primary motivation, I think thus far we can say they have succeeded in that.

As a consequence of that initial step, clearly economic issues became more and more and more important. And so my point was if you look at things on a straight line economic trajectory, then 3 years ago we could easily have seen the outcome of Europe, whether it was Greece-specific, Ireland-specific, Portugal-specific, or Europe-specific, would have ended in a very different set of circumstances because economically, under the political and legal constraints in play in the treaties and under the rules and regulations of Europe at the time, the outcome should have been much more daunting and dramatically bad. But political considerations stepped in and Europe ended up where they said they could not go—that is, there are a lot of the "we will never go there" points—for example, they all said that there will never be a point in which one country bails out another. There is an anti-bail-out clause in the treaties in Europe. Well, clearly, as I suggested in my testimony, there are now permanent and other mechanisms that are there for that very purpose. They are there through economic means, but to achieve the political purpose of keeping the European Union together and harmonized.

The CHAIRMAN. So when I have often thought of the European Union at its beginning, I thought of it as—I described it as, well, it is this club, so to speak, and there are high standards to be part of the club. And if you want to get a key to the club, you had to meet the high standards, and those countries that were not, in fact, capable of meeting those standards that the incipiency would have the assistance to be able to build themselves up to be able to meet those standards and therefore be part of the union. That is a very broad analogy.

Do you see that as the original intent, either one of you?

Mr. REDIKER. Yes, with a big "but," and the big "but" is there were a number of countries that could not meet that high standard in getting in. So the choice was either you remain wedded to an explicitly strict standard and say until you get here, you are just not coming in or, again back to my point about politics, there was a political decision taken that a number of countries that were not going to, anytime soon, meet that standard, that high standard, so how can we finesse their entry because it was better to have them in and encourage them along a productive, positive course rather than keep them out and wait and see when they got their act together sufficiently economically and politically to meet that high standard. So, again, yes, they set rules that were written in stone until they were not really written in stone.

Mr. KOLBE. I would agree with what Doug just said about the way in which the European Union has come about and the way in which it has evolved. As you look at the creation of the euro currency and the Eurozone, it is easy now to look back. And some people at the time said this was going to be the problem that they created with the European Central Bank. They centralized the finance, the monetary side of the picture, but they never really centralized the fiscal side of the picture. So you had the countries in the southern tier that were not as economically as well off, did not have the ability—or were almost induced to have more greater deficit spending because they were able to do that. The so-called 3-percent limit on the deficit—really there was no enforcement mechanism for it. But this all turned out, of course, to be to the advantage of the countries on the other side as well who were exporting all these goods to countries like Greece and Spain and Portugal and elsewhere. So it was a symbiotic relationship. Now they are trying to deal with that problem today, and it is going to be a very long time before, I think, they are able to work themselves out of this.

The CHAIRMAN. One final question. You know, emerging economies have become bigger players in the international economy and also in international governance. That, I think, is evidenced by the prominence of the G20. And at the same time, United States policy is now—we have this rebalancing toward Asia. We have an increasing interest in other parts of the world.

How does the importance of our economic relationship and economic cooperation with the Europeans rank in this evolving context where the slow growth European nations seem to be ceding their global economic leadership role to the faster growing emerging markets? And what economic issues would we benefit from—I think some you touched on in some of your original testimony—from a tighter, closer, more harmonized United States-European Union cooperation? I offer that question to both of you.

Mr. KOLBE. I will lead off with just a brief answer.

I think you have, in a sense, answered the question yourself. As I suggested in my remarks, the advantage of the TTIP is not the reduction of tariffs, which are as close to zero as any countries have in their trade relationship, though there still will be significant economic benefits by eliminating all the tariffs. Because of the sheer size of the trade relationship, eliminating those tariffs will have a significant benefit.

But the real benefits will come from the nontariff barriers. If we are able to resolve—and I say ''if''—the key things like the agricultural issues, the GMOs, the issue of procurement, which is a major issue for the Europeans here in the United States, the issue of automobile regulation and inspection, financial services, a major issue on both sides—if we are able to resolve those, the benefits will be tremendous.

The sheer size of this economic relationship will not harm our growing relationship with China and other Asian countries, but I think it will enhance the world's view as we look toward trying to bring Doha back into being again, the Doha Round of talks. This is a way, in a sense, to do that by having an agreement that other countries could join in. So it becomes kind of a bilateral plus a regional agreement that is much larger than that, and other countries can join into it.

Mr. REDIKER. Well, just picking up on Jim's point, I think I am less optimistic that we are ultimately going to get to something like a Doha because we have tried and it has become very clear how difficult it is.

But picking up on your initial question, what we, I think, have started to engage in are these super-regional agreements and alliances. These are not just individual bilateral trade agreements or investment agreements. These are very large and meaningful blocs that we are negotiating with now potentially whether it is Europe with TTIP or with Asia through TPP. That actually has enormous potential through these regional efforts to create the rules of the road both on the tariff basis in those countries in those areas where we still have high tariffs and in the nontariff areas where it is really regulatory and nontariff issues. That sets a framework that ultimately is one of those instances where—to be colloquial about it—we are saying, "I am not going to wait for you. I am moving ahead, and you can either hop on the train or you are going to be left behind."

And if we end up driving those, I certainly do not think it is Europe to the detriment of Asia or Asia to the detriment of Europe. I think we are in a unique position, in engaging in these two major potential agreements, to set those rules of the road which basically end up determining, whether countries like it or not, the rules of the rest of the world are going to end up having to deal with. So I think it is very positive.

I also think in terms of the fast growing, emerging markets versus the established, more developed markets of Europe, it is kind of a stocks-and-flows argument to some degree, meaning there is such a deep and embedded relationship commercially and trade- and investment-wise between the United States and Europe that although there are clearly huge growth opportunities in the emerging markets that we as a country are well served by embracing wholeheartedly, that is not to diminish the enormity of our relationship with Europe. So I think both are important. One is obviously faster growing; the other is just so deep and robust and long-term that we have to take it enormously seriously.

The CHAIRMAN. Thank you very much.

Senator Corker.

Senator CORKER. Thank you, Mr. Chairman, and each of you for your testimony and for being here.

I know you have talked of a greater engagement with the European Union. But the European Union has decided to be the European Union and it has gone through a lot of trials and tribulations. I know this is not for us to determine. But would you say that the success of the European Union is in our national interest versus a disparate group of countries operating independently?

Mr. KOLBE. Unquestionably, yes. The disintegration of the European Union, if that actually occurred, would be catastrophic to the United States and to our international interests, our political, economic, diplomatic interests. It would be very serious.

Mr. REDIKER. I would agree. I see only upside in the European Union staying together. I think if you get back to a very core premise of values, which both Congressman Kolbe and I referred to, the ideas of democracy, of consensus, of property rights—go on down the list of things that we as a country and as a people take as a basic foundation—are not necessarily accepted all around the world. So the fact that between ourselves and the European Union we have those basic shared values is an enormous starting point for any conversations on almost any subject in a multilateral or global context.

Mr. KOLBE. If I might just add to that. Were that worst case scenario that you described to occur, think what might happen to the Central and Eastern European countries that have gradually moved toward the European Union and toward democracy and an open market economic system. They would then be very vulnerable to being drawn back into a Russian orbit, and that cannot be good for the United States. It certainly cannot be good for democracy in the rest of the world or for the economic system.

Senator CORKER. I was interested to hear your comments about looking at the European Union through a political lens. Do you see it progressing on to become is a true fiscal union? Some of the problems have been solved through stop gap measures since the crisis, but will the European Union evolve further?

Mr. REDIKER. They are certainly progressing. And as I mentioned in my statement, it is painful to watch because getting 27 countries to agree on anything is very difficult, and that is just a starting point because it is not only the 27 countries, it is the institutions, it is the subgroups within the 27. It is enormously complicated and cumbersome.

I am worried that while they are progressing on the banking union, which is the first step in this next iteration of Europe, that there are some very difficult issues that are now coming to the fore. So they have kicked the can down the road sufficiently to get to where they are, and I applaud them for it. But some of the most difficult issues are now really ripe for being resolved.

And again, as I mentioned, I think that the difference between where the Germans start from and where some others—and particularly the French—start from is a case where it is not that these circles do not overlap at all, but it is hard to find the areas where you really can find areas of agreement on very fundamental issues.

Again, I will repeat. This comes down to the retention of national sovereignty versus ceding some of that to a central authority on financial matters and political matters. That is really tough existential stuff for these countries and their governments, and that is what lies ahead in the short term.

Senator CORKER. Can they survive over a 20-, 30-, or 40-year period without achieving greater fiscal unity?

Mr. REDIKER. I think what is urgently needed is a continuation of what we have seen largely via the European Central Bank, which is an ability to take weaker countries and banks where their financing dries up and find some way to mutualize that. Thus far, they have found ways to do that through the ECB, through these other mechanisms, the ESM, the EFSF, and others. Over time—and that is not a long period of time, your question was over a 20-, 30-, 40-year framework—this stop gap system is not sustainable. There needs to be some means by which a permanent resolution of these outstanding issues is arrived at.

And if you listen to what the Germans and others say, they say we are willing—much more willing than they were 3 years ago, mind you—to put our sovereign balance sheet at risk if you, whoever you are—collectively the rest of you, so to speak—agree to take certain steps to allow us to feel comfortable about what that risk really looks like. But that is really tough stuff because it does mean that loss of sovereignty at some level, and how they navigate through that is difficult.

So the short answer to your question is "No." If they do not resolve this over the short to medium term, I do not see it sustainable as within a 20-year timeframe. I would say it is not sustainable within a 5-to-10-year timeframe.

Senator CORKER. NATO has been a tremendous alliance for our security. On the other hand, there are only three European Union countries that are actually honoring their agreement on defense spending. What has really happened with NATO over time is we are the provider of protective services and they are the consumer of protective services. That cannot continue. And I am only slightly exaggerating when I say what I just said. Certainly there have been meaningful contributions. But over time, that is the way this has evolved.

Can you talk a little bit about the interrelationship between NATO and the fiscal union? We are talking about the TTIP agreement that we hope comes to a success and just overall security issues relative to NATO, which is very important to us on another front.

Mr. KOLBE. Well, just in a general way, your premise is certainly correct. We have been by far the largest contributor to NATO, and the other countries have not come up to the standard that has been set for the NATO countries in terms of their contributions of their budget to the NATO defense.

But I think it goes back to what we were both saying earlier in our remarks, and that is that the European Union is a political union, and these do all tie together. There is no question that these issues are interlinked. And it is hard to see if the European Union were to continue to fray and to show that it is coming apart at the seams—it is hard to see how we can have any resolution of the security issues.

I do think that the European Union and the integration, the economic and continuing political integration that it has, enables us to have greater cooperation with Europe on some of these security issues, whether it is in Libya and other parts of north Africa, whether it is in the Middle East. We have not had all the cooperation we would like, and we have not seen eye to eye on everything certainly in Afghanistan or Iraq. But we have had much greater cooperation than we would have had, I think, had we been trying to deal with 27 different countries on the economic front.

Senator CORKER. Mr. Chairman, is it all right if I keep going?

The issue of Turkey. I know Turkey is not part of the European Union. There have been issues there that have kept that from occurring. They are evolving into a more important country in terms of our national interest.

As we look at this TTIP negotiation that is taking place—I know Turkey's Prime Minister was here recently talking with the President about the trade agreement. How should we look at Turkey as we move ahead with TTIP? Are there bilateral discussions that ought to take place relative to them and this entire trade agreement?

Mr. REDIKER. I would not want to speculate on whether the Turkey conversation relative to trade is going to be a plus or a negative relative to TTIP. But I would bring the question back to Turkey and its overall strategic role economically and politically and say it is enormous and it has evolved considerably vis-a-vis the EU. So I would say within the last 5 to 10 years, the issue of Turkey joining the EU has stopped being a front page news story both in Turkey and across the European Union. It was a pretty important election campaign issue in the German and French elections the last go-round, meaning not this most recent but the previous one, and now is basically a nonissue. And in part it is a nonissue because the Turks have made it a nonissue because their clamoring to get into the EU has been quieted not only by the turmoil in the EU, but by their own sense of strategic importance in a role that they played which was somewhat unforeseen at the time. They felt 10 years ago that their future really needed to be anchored in the robust central political and economic health provided by the European Union. And over time, obviously, as the context of this hearing demonstrates, the European Union is not considered to be the magnet for economic growth in the future that it once was.

But more than that, Turkey plays this enormously interesting and strategic role of east-west—there are a variety of issues that we could go into in greater detail. But they actually feel much stronger now I am not saying as a stand-alone because as a stand-alone, that is overstating it. But certainly their sense of importance as an independent actor in the region militarily, security-wise, economically, tradewise is much deeper. And so they themselves are of, at best, two minds about whether they want to join the EU or not.

And in the context of trade, as I say, that is not an area I have looked at in great detail, but I would suggest that TTIP with Turkey added on would be—I am not going to say a bridge too far, but it is already going to be wildly difficult to get 27 countries to agree on most things. The Turkey issue, in the context of trade and TTIP, I would suggest, is probably one step beyond where we would like to go.

Mr. KOLBE. If I might just add to that. I agree with what Doug has just said about Turkey seeing itself today as a bigger player in the world and in the region. They see themselves as kind of at the center between Europe on one side, the Middle East on the other, north Africa, the former Russian bloc up here. They see themselves as playing a very strategic role, and they do. They always have from NATO. They have been a part of NATO from the very beginning.

I was just in Turkey last month and what I found in the conversations with them about TTIP is that they are concerned. They are concerned that they are going to get left out. Somehow they are going to get squeezed out of the talks, and somehow their trade relationship with Europe, which is quite substantial, much larger than their trade relationship with the United States—it is one of the things we should be focused on, increasing that trade relationship. They are worried about being left out of that or squeezed out of that. So they are very concerned about this. They do not expect that they are going to be made a part of it, though they say we have been a part of NATO all along. We have been there before all these other countries were. Why should we not be considered to be a part of it?

Senator CORKER. I just will ask one last question, if it is OK with the chairman.

I know that you all are very focused on TTIP and other issues. Is it your opinion, looking from the outside, that the administration seems to be fully committed to this and is doing all the things they need to do to bring this to fruition?

Mr. KOLBE. I would say "Yes." I mean, I do not think this administration would have gone down the path of starting the TTIP negotiation if they were not committed to getting it done, and I think the nomination of Mr. Froman to be the U.S. Trade Representative—he is deeply invested in this, and I think he clearly has a reason to see it through to the end. That is not, however, to gainsay the difficulties that are going to be involved in getting this agreement done. There are substantial and very deep differences over a number of issues that are going to be very tough to negotiate. So I think we have got a long road ahead of us.

One of the things that is a little bit of concern is that the Commission finds itself coming to an end in the middle of next year. They have a timetable that they would like to see this done by that time. That is unrealistic. And we are, of course, looking at the end of the Obama administration as a timetable for it. So kind of meshing these two timetables is going to be one of the first things that they are going to have to think about.

Senator CORKER. Thank you both and thank you, Mr. Chairman, for having this hearing.

The CHAIRMAN. Thank you, Senator Corker.

I just want to make two observations. One on the Turkey question. Obviously, part of the challenge is for the Europeans, in considering Turkey as an addition to a very difficult set of negotiations, is that everybody in the EU has agreed to live to a certain set of standards across the spectrum. And we have talked about some of those challenges of being able to achieve those standards. It would be easy to piggyback onto a negotiation but not have to live up to a whole set of standards. And I think that is probably one of the challenges at the end of the day.

And the other is that I think this is the first time the committee has had a hearing as a full committee on Europe in over 2 years. I think it is an expression of the importance that we have that we view of the United States-European relationship, particularly the

European Union. And we look forward to continuing to deepen those understandings through the committee's work as well.

With the thanks of the committee to both of you for your insights, the record will remain open until Friday of this week for questions that members would have.

This hearing is adjourned.

[Whereupon, at 11:45 a.m., the hearing was adjourned.]

ADDITIONAL MATERIAL SUBMITTED FOR THE RECORD

RESPONSE OF UNDER SECRETARY ROBERT HORMATS AND UNDER SECRETARY LAEL
BRAINARD TO QUESTION SUBMITTED BY SENATOR CHRISTOPHER A. COONS

Question. As we seek closer trade ties with Europe, it is important that we ensure a level playing field through the even application of the European Union (EU) regulatory process. While the EU has initiated a number of commendable environmental regulations, not all Member States properly comply. This can disadvantage U.S. companies which have invested in reliance on the anticipated implementation of the regulation. For example, a variety of U.S. companies have made investments, many of them quite significant, related to implementation of the Mobile Air Conditioning, or MAC, Directive. The Directive was scheduled to go into effect at the beginning of the year, but there are increasing reports of widespread noncompliance. The U.S. companies who made good faith investments based on the Directive are now experiencing economic harm.

• What steps is the administration taking to ensure U.S. companies are able to compete in a fair and consistent process?

Answer. We are consulting closely within the interagency and with the European Commission (and, as needed, with EU Member States) on regulatory issues, including the Mobile Air Conditioning (MAC) directive. In our discussions with the Europeans, we have stressed the importance to U.S. companies that this directive be implemented properly on an EU-wide basis so that shortcomings in implementation do not undermine investments that companies have already made. We will continue to raise this issue and the importance for our trading relationship of having all EU Member States apply EU directives in a timely and consistent manner. Eliminating disparate Member State implementation of and compliance with EU legislation is an important component of our engagement through the Transatlantic Trade and Investment Partnership (TTIP) to reduce regulatory barriers to trade and ensure a level playing field for U.S. companies.

RESPONSE OF UNDER SECRETARY ROBERT HORMATS TO QUESTION SUBMITTED BY
SENATOR JEANNE SHAHEEN

Question. In your testimony you mention that upcoming trade negotiations with respect to the Transatlantic Trade and Investment Partnership (TTIP) will aim to address "behind the border" barriers to U.S.-EU trade, including "unnecessary regulatory and standards differences that create burdens for our exporters, while maintaining appropriate health, safety, and environmental protections."

Both sides of the Atlantic are in the process of determining their mandate for the upcoming negotiations. One of the longstanding sticking points will be regulatory differences and compatibility issues.

• With respect to possible regulatory harmonization in the upcoming TTIP negotiations, which sectors do you anticipate will provide the best opportunity for U.S. businesses to benefit from a TTIP deal?
• Which sectors, if any, will the United States trade negotiators push to remove from consideration with respect to regulatory harmonization discussions?
• Do you anticipate that the medical technology and medical device technology industries will be covered under the upcoming TTIP negotiations? What is the possibility for convergence on the regulatory front with respect to medical technology and medical device technology exports?

Answer. As indicated in the High-Level Working Group report and in the United States Trade Representative's March 20 notification letter to Congress on the Transatlantic Trade and Investment Partnership (TTIP), one of our major negotiating objectives will be to find ways to remove "behind the border" barriers to trade and to address regulatory restrictions that impose costs, reduce efficiencies, and limit the ability of firms on both sides of the Atlantic to compete and innovate. Our goal is to establish strong horizontal disciplines that will benefit all sectors. With respect to sector-specific regulatory issues and regulatory cooperation, the administration's Trade Policy Staff Committee is currently analyzing public inputs received in response to USTR's Federal Register notice. We will have a better sense of the areas where progress is most possible and where there are potential roadblocks later this summer once negotiations have commenced.